ANITA WILLIS

Build *It* Beyond

From a *dream* to
a *vision* for your life

© 2022 Anita Willis

info@builditbeyond.com

www.BuildItBeyond.com

build_it beyond_anitawillis

Anita Dawn Willis

Anita Willis IBH

@builditbeyond

Interior by Brenda Hawkes

Cover Design by JJAC Graphics, LLC

Editorial direction by Anne Bruce and Phyllis Jask

Printed in the United States of America

ISBN-979-8-9855076-6-9

Contents

There comes a point in each person's life where they have to make the choice to Build it Beyond. Whether that time is now or later, this book has found its way into your life, which means there is purpose for it. Author Anita Willis masterfully takes her life experiences that led to her success and shares her message to help you Build it Beyond. The book takes four foundational pillars to help you recognize your truth, accept your truth, embrace your worth, and build your platform.

Each one of these tools is essential to embrace as you choose to find and recognize the core of who you are, starting with recognizing your truth. This principle is essential for anyone who wants to Build It Beyond. Not knowing the truth of who you are creates a faulty foundation that keeps you in unhealthy cycles of life. However, she takes you further by challenging you to not just know it, but to accept your truth. Using very practical and relevant stories and exercises, you will be able to dive deeper into your journey, which ultimately leads to embracing your worth.

As a licensed professional counselor and certified coach, I have come to understand that many people find it hard to embrace their worth based on traumas past and future. However, it is only when you embrace your worth that you can fully commit to building your platform. Anita does an exceptional job at sharing not just information, but insight that gives you a chance to build a platform not just for yourself, but those you will come in contact with!

Jump in and prepare for the journey as you choose to Build it Beyond.

—Dr. Arthur W. Tigney, Jr., Ed.D., M.A., LPC

Preface

*B*y the grace of God, I've had some ups and downs in life and love. Haven't we all? But with every challenge I've encountered, I've learned how to Build It Beyond. With every misstep I've tripped over, I've discovered the power within me to embrace a bold and beautiful life. And so can you.

What's that even mean—Build It Beyond? As for me, it means recognizing where I am and what got me there to begin with, then acknowledging my truth for what it really is (and not manipulating it into my perception of what I think it is). Knowing this, I can make a plan to create change to live the life of my dreams with no apologies and no excuses.

I believe you can, too. You see, change can also be seen as a memorable acronym: Challenged to Hear the Advantages Necessary for Growth and Excellence. When you accept the challenge to hear your truth, you're growing. Agile change often begins when you accept your truths, and when you truly listen and take to heart what's being said. It's more than listening. It's hearing the deeper meaning of the message being sent. It's called deep listening.

My advice—start where you are. Every time in my life when I've had to start over—and it's not a one-time occurrence—I've had to think about the choices I made that got me there in the first place. Let's face it, everybody makes mistakes. Some decisions are winners and keep you on the right path. Those are the easy ones.

Sometimes the results of good decisions end up being huge mistakes. And some hurt more than others. Way more. Only by being honest with myself and facing the hard truths, disappointment, misjudging others' character, shame, humiliation, frustration, or heartbreak did I recognize that some mistakes and all consequences were mine to address, and mine alone. Admitting mistakes requires self-honesty, self-awareness, and self-forgiveness. And for some of us, being absolutely honest with ourselves is a pretty big hill to climb. But I learned early on when I saw my truths for what they were could I embrace them and start rebuilding from there. The question I learned to ask myself was this: how do I walk from here? That's a lesson for us all. To achieve better results for every moment, you must chunk it down to your basics, and listen for the path and look for the light you need to walk your journey.

Change of any kind can be intimidating at first. But just like climbing a mountain, eating the frog, starting a journey, or whatever cliché you prefer, you take it one step at a time. I began by breaking it down to the core of who I am—taking a deep dive into what makes me tick. Among my core values is my faith. I am blessed by a strong faith that carries me through hard times and keeps me up during good times. I trust that I'll know what to do because I believe God guides me with the wisdom I need to believe in myself and in my purpose and endeavors. When things are dark and trying, it's difficult to *listen* for answers when looking for answers seems easier. However, leaning into my faith helps me quiet myself so I can hear. No matter what situation I find myself in, I've learned it is through prayer and meditation that I lean into my faith, quiet my mind, and silence my doubts. My faith toward God helps me to listen, receive, and accept so I can live my truth. Only with honesty and clarity, could I achieve my life and career goals in the face of sometimes overwhelming adversities.

I didn't write this book to tell you how to live your life. That's not what I'm about. I am, however, about encouraging, inspiring, and uplifting you to a prosperous soulful and spiritual level. Here is where you might learn some things from how

I have navigated through my own challenges and mistakes. Adapt my lessons into ones you can use to Build It Beyond for yourself and then expand those lessons for ongoing and continuous personal and professional development. I've got your back.

I believe this book will help you to discover your inner honesty, clarity, passion, and purpose. I promise to give it to you straight—no chaser.

Introduction

*W*e are living in unprecedented times, having
experienced global pandemic, economic unrest,
and long overdue recognition of racial inequality
and inequities in the United States where I live,
as well as worldwide. We are one human race and
these realities touch us all. People everywhere are
experiencing drastic, insurmountable changes and
challenges thrust upon them, and I'll tell you, it's
hard to manage life when you have a million burdens
on your shoulders at once. How do you rise up and
recalibrate when the cards are stacked against you?

Inside each of us resides a solid core of strength. After
life knocks you down, you can use the strength you

already have in yourself to propel you toward your personal and professional goals. You've just got to find—then tap into—that strength to hit those goals. Every time I've faced adversity in my life, I discovered my own strength I'd forgotten I'd had all along. Of course, it is an incontestable fact that there's value in experiential knowledge. I had to quit listening to the voice of reasoning inside my head and steel my resolve to do better in order to be the best person that I could be in that moment. When the birthing or memory of a time in your life becomes a barrier and better than the baby, something's got to change. And that something is your mindset—how you perceive your own strength despite your circumstances. The decision becomes do you lay in this misery or make it a purpose-filled memory? This becomes that moment where the lesson is not taught, but rather it's caught.

I remember the moment I thought of *Build It Beyond: From a Dream to a Vision for Your Life*. Inspired by my mother, I could hear her words in my ear: *You are bigger than your troubles. I've never*

seen anyone who refuses to quit even when down,
you always come back no matter what. That was all
the reminder I ever needed to take a much needed
pause, grieve the loss, pick myself up, and get busy
fulfilling the dreams embedded within the vision for
my life.

I call it the Rhythm of Grace—I've always had it and
so do you. Rhythm of Grace is recognizing that when
you are worn down from the journey, you can give
yourself grace and not beat yourself up with giver's
remorse, because of your missteps or misdeeds, even
your good deeds gone wrong. Accept responsibility
for your actions—both good and bad—then move on,
wiser for having had the experience in the first place
where you discover there is truth within the trials.
It's different for each person and each situation.
It's asking yourself "How do *I* feel about that?"
and answering your own question truthfully—*and
without judgment.* Then you identify what tools
you've overlooked and those you need that you don't
currently have so you can improve your situation.

Everyone lives their own experience. Mine may be similar to yours, but your experience is yours alone. You direct your story when you turn your focus away from your pain and toward building beyond your past breaking points, and your last mental, social, or emotional limitation. It's what helps us move through life into new territory, experiences, and memories.

In these pages you'll learn how to walk from here in the present, think from here, and go from here. You'll learn to quiet your mind so you can listen, recognize every moment isn't one of death but can be one of growth. You'll discover your own transformation depending on your situation, and you'll learn there is no growth without discomfort, and discomfort comes with growth. The choice to move forward is always yours.

There is no growth without discomfort, and discomfort comes with growth.

Build It Beyond was created on four key foundational pillars:

- Recognize Your Truth
- Accept Your Truth
- Embrace Your Worth
- Build Your Platform

Part One: *Recognize Your Truth opens you up to awakening to and exploring your core values.* You've always known who you are and what values guide your decisions; you just may not have acknowledged it before. What do you stand for? You can't build on a faulty foundation. What is your inborn temperament and what causes your knee-jerk reactions? What are your cooperative environments or non-negotiable boundaries? Recognizing your core values—supported by your truth—helps you find your way back on track if you've lost your way, and helps you listen to your own voice to find your resolve. Recognizing your truth helps you to break through and break into new opportunities rather than break down in times of trouble.

Part Two: *Accept Your Truth explores knowing the value of your value.* How you cope with big changes—health, job, economic, relationship, etc.—is defined by how you personify and accept your core values. How you work toward your personal and professional goals after your world has drastically changed, how you change with it all and roll with the punches, and where you go from here, all hinge on you. You're the common denominator in your life. You'll learn how to adapt this into an ongoing practice in your life until it emerges as a vital part of your lifestyle.

Part Three: *Embrace Your Worth uncovers how and with whom you share your value is a reflection of your thoughts, patterns, and ingrained behaviors.* It's okay to be selective with whom you share your pearls of wisdom. Not everyone is the right audience at the right time, and you don't have to be all things to all people. Take the time to trust yourself and love yourself into a new way of thinking that aligns with your core values and healthy choices, mindset, and lifestyle.

Part Four: *Build Your Platform is where the rubber meets the road.* You're making your personal values equation by using your core values to guide the actions you take to improve and move forward with your life. You can create a cooperative environment by reframing how you approach a challenge, and adopt your values equation by adding an abundance mindset to aid in your continued growth. Building your platform also requires that you practice self-care. Self-care is not selfish; it is critical to understanding the value of your value and how you show up every day.

Throughout the book, I share my personal experiences and how I used these lessons, tools, and strategies to release my inner strength. I also include strategy-building exercises that will challenge your current thinking to help you identify your values, accept your reality, learn self-care, and acknowledge when you need help.

Always keep in mind, though, that these strategies don't work **_unless you do the work_**. I'll show you how to trust your inner truth so you can apply your values on every level of your life, but you've got to put in the effort, face your strengths and shortcomings, then resolve to move forward because really, what better choice do you have? Would you rather stay comfortable and stuck where you are, or do you really want to Build It Beyond and move from merely dreaming about your best life to living the vision you have for it?

I'm living proof the tools and strategies I outline on these pages work. I've spent a lifetime beta-testing and fine-tuning them. Now it's your time to prosper.

Part One:

Recognize
Your Truth

*T*o Build It Beyond, you begin by exploring
your core values. Recognizing who you are, what
you stand for, and what your inborn temperament
might be are crucial to building your self-awareness.
You can't build on a faulty foundation. When you
know who you are and what your values are, even
in tough times when the world around you seems to
crumble, you can stand strong in the knowledge that
you know what you need to do.

Deep down inside, you may already know what
your core values are, but you just may not have
acknowledged them and used them consciously to
guide your decisions. And if you've never thought
about them before, the time to start is now.

Recognizing your truth helps you find your way
back on track if you've lost your way. And we all do.
Listen to your inner voice of wisdom to find your

resolve because when you recognize your truth, you are better equipped to break through and break into new opportunities—rather than break down—in times of trouble.

You are worthy of the time it takes for your own personal discovery.

Being true to yourself and identifying your core values is critical, because *your personal truth stems from the willingness to be honest and transparent with yourself on how we really show up for ourselves.*

Your willingness to question "Is it enough?" or "Can I show up better?" can be the tipping point for inner transformation that trigger the soul-work required to cultivate truthfulness within yourself.

The knowing and the unknowing rests in personal authenticity and trust. Can you be trusted to walk out the change needed to realize the vision you have for your life?

At a deeper level, personal authenticity and trust connects to your core values because it always leads to your behavior and reveals your personal character. How you behave demonstrates the values you hold dear and allows you to live your truth to the best of your ability and personal integrity.

Being true to yourself is more difficult than it appears. Most people will say one thing and do another. But you cannot behave in a way that is not in alignment with how you ultimately see yourself. It's your opinion or vision of yourself that matters most. When you learn to combine your personal authenticity, trust, and truth with your core values consistently, a transformative imprint takes place in how you think and envision life for yourself. This is how you will Build It Beyond. How do you know it's right? It feels right. It's the ultimate mindset you will uphold and establish for yourself with no regret.

Identify Your Core Values

Who are you? No, really, *who are you*? What do you stand for? What's the moral code you live by? Without a solid foundation of values and morals to follow, you're going through life rudderless, just floating directionless along with the tides, not getting where you really want to go and accepting the belief that settling for where you are is good enough. It's easy to go with the flow of what society or media deems valuable and fooling yourself that the values of others are the right values for you.

Values such as integrity, honesty, self-improvement, self-respect, grace, open-mindedness, dependability, reliability, self-discipline, courage, unselfishness, and countless others guide your decisions. Values are as varied as people. The values you commit to consistently reveal to others your character—not the other way around. A collection of your decisions over the course of your life has landed you where you are and can set the course for where you go in the future. In order to Build It Beyond, you've first got to recognize where you are starting and what you are starting with. Discover what being you means to *you*.

Discover what being you means to you.

Do you know your "why"? Your "why" is the reason behind your decisions—literally the "why" you do what you do and how you do it. Your "why" should be guided by and based on your core values. Because, like the saying goes, if you don't stand for something, you'll fall for anything. Your "why" matters because it is the shadow of who you were yesterday, who you are today, and who you'll become in the future.

Identifying, accepting, and living your core values is at the heart of true and genuine personal authenticity. It frees you to run your race as the person you are and live your authentic life. When you base your decisions and act accordingly on your core values, you are aligning your actions with your beliefs. Your core values lift you up when you're down and keep you up when you're up. We often model our morals and core values based on what we've grown up with or what we've become accustomed to. Many of us were blessed to grow up with caregivers who modeled a strong set of values, and we learned our values system from them. We also adopt value traits of those who we admire and respect.

To live your values is to know yourself.

However, there are many others among us for whom chaos and dysfunction were the norm. How do you know when you're living in dysfunction? This can happen when your original beliefs cease to serve the person you've become, when you start to question why you're doing what you're doing, and when you no longer find truth within nor are fulfilled by your actions. The habits that we form over a lifetime should reflect our core values because we can't build a good life and make smart decisions based on a faulty values foundation. We also can't build a good life for ourselves when we're living according to someone else's values or past experiences. When you ask yourself questions like "Do my actions reflect my values?" and "Am I letting others' opinions and advice compromise my values?" and answer honestly and truthfully, you are acknowledging your inner truth and expressing self-love and self-respect. To live your values is to know yourself.

Identify Your Core Values Exercise

Write, journal, pray, meditate, or just think deeply about the following list of values to help you create a list of the values that are most important to you. Feel free to add others, too.

- Achievement
- Ambition
- Authenticity
- Awareness
- Balance
- Beauty
- Boldness
- Bravery
- Brilliance
- Calm
- Candor
- Charity
- Commitment
- Common sense
- Communication
- Community
- Compassion
- Competency
- Confidence
- Connection
- Consciousness
- Consistency
- Courage
- Creativity
- Credibility
- Curiosity
- Dedication
- Dependability
- Determination
- Discipline
- Efficiency
- Empathy
- Enthusiasm
- Equality
- Ethical
- Excellence
- Fairness
- Faith
- Family
- Fortitude
- Freedom
- Friendship
- Fun
- Generosity
- Good humor
- Goodness
- Grace
- Gratitude
- Happiness
- Health
- Honesty
- Honor
- Hope
- Humility

- Individuality
- Inner harmony
- Innovation
- Inspiring
- Integrity
- Intelligence
- Intuition
- Justice
- Kindness
- Knowledge
- Leadership
- Lifelong learning
- Love
- Loyalty
- Meaningful work
- Motivation
- Open-mindedness
- Optimism
- Organization
- Originality
- Passion
- Performance
- Perseverance
- Persistence
- Personal development
- Playfulness
- Positivity
- Power
- Productivity
- Professionalism
- Purpose
- Quality
- Recognition
- Reliability
- Respect
- Responsibility
- Reverence
- Risk
- Security
- Self-control
- Self-esteem
- Self-love
- Self-care
- Selfless
- Self-respect
- Self-worth
- Service
- Sincerity
- Spirituality
- Stability
- Success
- Temperance
- Thankfulness
- Tolerance
- Transparency
- Trustworthiness
- Vision
- Vitality
- Wealth
- Welcoming
- Well-being
- Wisdom

You can accomplish big changes by starting with small steps. Write your top 12 values in the lines below. By focusing on one value each month of the year, you can further identify your core values and how you apply them to your daily life:

January: _____

February: _____

March: _____

April: _____

May: _____

June: _____

July: _____

August: _____

September: _____

October: _____

November: _____

December: _____

Now, think about a profound positive and a profound negative experience from your life. What values did you learn through both those positive and negative experiences? What values did you honor or ignore in making those decisions? What did you learn about your character through these times?

Acknowledge which values take precedence in your current circumstances. Sometimes you'll be in a situation where your values conflict. For example, you have to decide between meeting a deadline (Productivity) and meeting a friend to catch up (Connection).

Next, write a statement that includes as many of the key words that apply to you, so that when completed you have framed a personal value equation that resonates with you and establishes how you express your core values into the world around you.

Acknowledge Your Temperament

I learned the value of understanding temperament years ago as I was raising my daughter Anna. I will always remember the day I sat my middle schooler down and explained the benefits of the boundaries that parents set for their children.

Anna was focused, headstrong, direct, and thrived on social interaction. Even at a young age, Anna had influence and still does today. She enjoyed a challenge and once it was over, she retreated like a hermit and would need time to build the energy to take her next big leap. Her challenges arose when I placed boundaries around her behavior because she wasn't understanding my mindset to protect her as a growing tween. My challenge during her development was to guide her "choleric" and "sanguine" responses, not squash them. As her mother, I am more "melancholy," or laid back and introverted in social interactions, and "supine," wired to serve others. For individuals like me who are melancholy, being in control of others in social situations is not in our comfort zone! I'd rather curl up with a book and nice cup of tea than to push myself to go out and be among people. Anna and I were total opposites. Knowing our temperaments assisted me as a parent to help her navigate her thoughts and behaviors regarding boundaries for time management, social activities, and consideration for others.

You might be wondering, "Huh? What are 'choleric,' 'sanguine,' 'melancholy,' and 'supine'?" I'll explain those in a bit, but first I want to explain what temperament is and how it influences your interactions with and perceptions of your environment. Knowing your temperament does not label you. It actually creates a freedom for you to grow and learn what to do to build healthier relationships, communication, and self-esteem.

The temperaments are melancholic, phlegmatic, sanguine, choleric, and supine, named for the "wisdom" of ancient times that based medical treatments on the balance of humors in our bodies. Now, thankfully modern science and medical knowledge have advanced well beyond the centuries, but the old-world temperament names stuck. People's temperaments are sometimes visible, but remember, they don't tell a person's entire story. Each temperament espouses different qualities in general, and should not be interpreted as good or bad.

- **Melancholic:** introverted, cautious, private, detail- and quality-oriented, logical, analytical, anxious, conscientious, tentative, rule follower, slow to trust others

- **Phlegmatic:** introverted, easy-going, calm, agreeable, patient, routine-oriented, resistant to change, passive or indecisive, works with others to achieve common goals, loyal, service-oriented

- **Sanguine:** extroverted, people-oriented, outgoing, optimistic, talkative, social, friendly, energetic, playful, impulsive, can be overwhelming to other temperament types, competitive

- **Choleric:** extroverted, results- and goal-oriented, driven, positive, self-confident, independent, strong-willed, assertive, direct, creative, domineering, opinionated, controlling

- **Supine:** introverted, responder rather than initiator, service-oriented, endearing, kind to a fault, empathetic, intuitive, tender-hearted

Do you see yourself in any of these descriptions? No person is 100 percent one temperament all the time—the uniqueness of your personal temperament can also be a blend in any one of these areas. Temperament is a spectrum that's used to aid understanding of your thought process and responses. Different interactions in different situations equals different experiences. Acknowledging your temperament helps you clarify how you respond to others socially and emotionally, and how easily you might be affected by external or internal influences.

The magic of understanding the temperament of others is helpful, too, and allows you to better gauge your reactions and responses, building long-lasting fruitful relationships, and in some cases avoiding pitfalls of unfruitful ones. Developing a deeper understanding of these characteristics can help you bring out your own best and also help you connect your values to your current situation so you can learn to create a cooperative environment by working around the extremes in others. You don't want to miss out on a life-changing experience because you are not sensitive to your temperament and that of others, and you write off an experience because of how you perceive it, or how others perceive you.

Anna, or "Muffin" as I affectionately called her, required the room to take charge without feeling guilty or lording over others. Offering direction for a take-charge child or individual is not domination at all; nevertheless, it feels that way to them. I explained that her take-charge manner is what would fuel her dynamic evolution as a great leader. As she began her journey, however, I wanted to make certain she understood the importance of knowing where her boundaries were and how they would benefit her in her relationship with me, her friends, and other adults. Once I explained that she was innocent without judgment and had loads of choices available and opportunity to make those independent choices, she was on her way!

You can make all the decisions within one hundred percent of the space that you have. I was affirming about her temperament and attempted to understand her emotionally; she felt in control and became more apt to share what was going on in "her world" as she was living it. Our conversation grew from a clashing in our temperaments to her accepting my supportive guidance and loving intent. The peace in the midst of the storm took place because I chose to respect and honor the boundaries of my own temperament and also those that I established for her health safety and well-being. I learned to love my daughter differently than what I expected for myself.

***

A November 2000[1] profile system theorized interpersonal relationships using three areas of interaction—inclusion, control, and affection—as they pertain to temperament. Inclusion is our inner

1 The Arno- Profile-System source:https://www.ncca.org/

drive to establish and maintain social relationships
with others, and it can work two ways: wanting
to be included by others and consideration for
others. Included within the sphere of inclusion is
the intellectual energy we use in social situations.
Control is our interpersonal need to take charge,
or make decisions and accept responsibility for
ourselves and/or others. Some people's self-concept
regarding control leans toward being responsible
and competent (as opposed to seeking power),
whereas others lean toward being trusting, respectful,
and willing to serve. Finally, there's affection; our
internal drive to either give or receive affection
determines how we experience an event through the
lens of how it makes us feel rather than by what we
accomplish. Expressing and receiving love, affection,
and approval including the need for deep personal
relationships is only scratching the surface, but you
get the idea. When someone falls on the extreme side
of a temperamental trait, it might explain any issues
with behavior, performance, or social interaction.

Knowing my own temperament has been priceless in
my life and in personal and professional interactions.

Having a baseline of phlegmatic and supine in affection, I am in love with love! (I'm laughing as I am writing this!) Love has to be the best emotion in the universe. However, over the years I never believed anyone would love me and if they did, they would eventually abandon me. Guess what? They did. Through accepting my personal truths, I learned that my filters found me excellent results that matched my self-limiting beliefs. All I could see is what I was thinking and believing about myself. Learning more about my temperament fueled my passion to live past my self-limitations. It's true, where your focus is, there lies your treasure. Only my treasure chest was filled with loving kindness that no one knew existed except through my "comfort zone" of service.

My service to others reframed my true intentions of being in a loving relationship that would lead to marriage because I equated the satisfaction of serving to loving others. It's the place where love became a limit. I sought support through temperament counseling where being worthy to be loved and return love became my new default for the way that I thought about love and affection.

It may not be this way for you. Maybe it takes too much energy for you to ask for love, like it was for me, and maybe you have a high need but low energy and find it exhausting. Finding out is the key to moving forward so you can Build It Beyond your last limiting thought and behavior. I can attest openly and honestly that I still love being in love, and with that I understand the work it takes to build a healthy relationship because the two are not the same.

You are worthy to make the change you want; you have the ability to do the work to get there by learning more about what you think, feel, and desire. The game plan for responding to affection or sharing affection goes way beyond the physical and rests within your willingness to change your mind—and by doing so, you will certainly change your choices.

Get to know the person you are when nobody else is in the room.

Another example I have is one of my coaching clients who found himself on the opposite side of the room during an argument with his wife. They had concerns that were not related to their love for one another but rather were business oriented. Knowing their temperament and observing their manner with one another during a coaching session, I realized they had taken physical positioning in the room that reflected their distance from one another emotionally and spiritually. Their spirituality played a huge role in their value equation, and was directly linked to their willingness to forgive and show compassion toward one another. Yet, both were in temperaments that were low in energy to seek affection (phlegmatic, supine) and high in energy to control the situation (choleric). What they wanted for one another they didn't know how to get it to each other.

I stood in between them like a referee in a boxing ring and asked these simple questions: "What do you want and what are you afraid of?" Both shared a similar variation of, "I don't want to be rejected and I need to have you near me." Because both were of phlegmatic temperament (low energy to express affection), the thing they needed most was touch, not talk. Learning how you function emotionally and mentally, and doing your work to clarify your social inclusion, control, and affection expressions in temperament liberates you to share more and better hear the needs and wants of others as well as yourself.

Knowing and appreciating individual differences helps you understand yourself and others more clearly. You'll gain insight about your temperament relative to the social energy you put out, your willingness to ask for what you want, and the energy you have to go after it. Get to know the person you are when nobody else is in the room. Learn what it takes for you to own the room and engage the people who are in it as well. Regardless of your temperament, it doesn't mean you can't make an effort to understand situations and people through a different lens. It just takes practice and patience.

Acknowledge Your Temperament Exercise

How would knowing your temperament help you to know yourself better, and invite others to know you as well?

Where do you see yourself falling on the spectrum and do you feel peace and fulfillment giving or receiving in the following areas?

- **Inclusion:** social interactions and intellectual energy used in these situations

- **Control:** your willingness to make decisions and to accept responsibility for yourself and/or others

- **Affection:** the need to express and receive love, affection, and approval; the need for deep personal relationships

Reflect on how others influence you and how you influence others. Strengthen your relationships by acknowledging your strengths and supporting your weaknesses. Take action to learn more about yourself in this area.

If you're unsure of your temperament, you can also take any number of online assessments or go to my website to schedule a temperament assessment and profile analysis.

Face Life's Pressures

I have heard it said that you know who you are when you are under pressure. How you respond to life's challenges paves the way for your future, shows what you're made of and how much grit you have, and reflects your character. How you tackle life's pressures is as unique as you are. Some might confront a challenging situation head on, whereas others might seek help or refuge first. There's no right answer. How you respond to pressure should be driven by your core values.

I believe that we should use the pressures we experience to learn from and come out with a heart filled with praise and gratitude. And that takes a certain amount of flexibility and open-mindedness. Now, I'm not saying we should rejoice in any loss or sorrow we feel when we experience difficulties, but we should learn from our experiences and use them to steel our resolve, recognize our applied strength, and build our resilience for the future.

Take a natural disaster like a storm, for example. We're warned to prepare our homes with flashlights and candles, bottled water and nonperishable food, and extra blankets to keep us warm, or if it's a really strong one, we're instructed to evacuate and seek refuge in a safe place. But, why wait? There are always going to be pressures, or "storms" in our lives. Preparing ourselves ahead of time is the best way to endure any storm life throws our way. We're always better off when we take action to plan for what we need before an event occurs. When you plan for pressures, you have a good idea of what to do when you're in the thick of it and generally know how to keep yourself moving forward afterward. Whatever pressures you are facing are real to you. Do not minimize them. Accept them for what they really are, and use your core values to create a plan to get beyond them. Your consistent use of your core values reflect your character. Acknowledging the consistency in your character to yourself empowers your self-concept and confirms positive self-leadership. I have often said, when you change your mind, you change your choices. The best choice you can make in advance is to have consistency of character and a community who supports your values and success.

When you change your mind, you change your choices.

Having consistency of character when the pressure is on is a kindness not only to yourself but to others. Your values are the guide to your not being blinded by emotion or panic when the pressure gets strong enough that you feel crushed by it. Your values equation gives you a sense of control, conscious awareness, and guides you where to go next and how you show up when you arrive.

The pressures you endure can make you stronger, and can even make you grateful for learning lessons from the experience. But most of all, they prove you can endure. In the midst of pressure, it's often difficult to believe anything good can come out of it, but it's critical to keep an open mind and be flexible in your journey through challenging times. During a difficult time in my life, I was injured in a car accident and couldn't work, which ultimately led to me returning my car to the manufacturer. I'll tell you, the anguish, disappointment, and embarrassment I felt were real. I had to depend upon others to travel, and it opened my heart to see beyond losing my car. I formed new and exciting relationships! Those new relationships became vital to strengthening my business foundation and my personal and academic achievements that year. I am certain that the advancements I experienced would not have happened to the degree they did had I been isolated in the privacy of my own car, alone without the people who were essential in shaping my path and my process. How I reframed my perspective of losing my car changed how I viewed my situation from a negative into a positive.

It's up to you to reframe how you view pressure. Instead of seeing pressures and challenges as something that can defeat you, instead discover and take advantage of the opportunities this challenging, pressure-filled world has thrust upon you. Reimagining the situation will help reframe your perspective.

In reframing your viewpoint from mourning "only" over what you have lost into seeing the situation as an opportunity, you put yourself into a place of conscious awareness about the next steps that will leave an imprint upon how you think about your life. Let go and embrace the time and ride the winds of change to discover what remains and what is now available to Build It Beyond what you have experienced. It is difficult but well worth the effort and the results. Discover what it feels like to be intentional about winning in the face of loss. I call it being rescued by the wind.

I remember a time of critical reflection that required me to take a trip home to Detroit. As I drove through my old neighborhood, it seemed forsaken and destroyed. Where our family home once stood was only the foundation, staircase, a single doorway, and mailbox. What a sight to see all my memories reduced to relics and ruins. I sat in front of what was once my home and heard these words: "Build upon the foundation and not the ruins." The wisdom of God in that moment whispered a life-changing opportunity to move forward with everything I needed to succeed. Many of you have had similar experiences as well. I say the same to you: Build upon the foundation and not the ruins.

How you react to pressure should be based on how you live your core values. Remember, your core values are your shelter and strength when you're in the middle of a storm. Your values become a light and a lamp on your path of renewal and restoration. You will be able to walk from here and Build It Beyond.

Facing Life's Pressures Exercise

Recall the previous exercise and the profound experience you had. If you had to do it over again, how can you reimagine the situation and reframe your perspective in order to apply your core values to make a different decision? Could you have developed a plan beforehand that could have guided a different outcome?

How can you adjust what didn't work so you don't repeat past mistakes in the future? What new boundaries would you establish to ensure your character plan supports how you want to show up every day?

Take action on your access. Identify family and friends you can trust and get their take on "how others see you." Do you agree or disagree with their impressions? These are the results of your decisions that leave a consistent imprint on others over time.

In other words, if the results are not what you want any longer, then you must change your thinking and behavior.

Find Your Way Back

How to find your way if you've lost it? It's easy to get discouraged when life's storms rain down upon you. You may feel out of control, directionless, hopeless, lethargic, unhappy. I get it because I've also been there. As for me, I use my core values of faith in God paired with my personal values equation to guide my decisions. For you it may be different.

No matter what your faith or guidance system is, I've noticed a few steadfast truths that can be helpful in finding your way toward living from a dream to a vision for your life again. First and foremost, you must have a life vision that ignites passion for living forward.

Have a heart-to-heart conversation with yourself: Be honest and truthful. Do not distort facts to suit how you wish to view your situation no matter how dire it is. Are you in the situation you're in because of decisions you made in the past? Did you not work as hard as you could have and now you're experiencing mediocre results? Stop rationalizing and making excuses. Don't pretend things are fine when they're anything but. It's a bitter pill to swallow when we admit to ourselves that a good decision has gone bad, or we messed up and are now suffering because of it. Nobody likes to admit they're wrong or admit someone we've trusted and valued in some way has let us down. Clarify your voice of compassion for yourself and apologize to yourself and mean it. No one wakes up and with intention of throwing themselves over a proverbial cliff. If this is you, admit that you are innocent of fault, but accountable for change. Then do something about it. Once you come clean with yourself, you can re-evaluate what got you there in the first place, then you can formulate a plan to improve your situation, perspective, perception, and most of all your mindset. Remember, change your mind to change your choices.

Abandon self-pity: It's not helpful. Self-pity creates a mindset suitable for complaining, rehearsing old times, rehashing old excuses, and can even become menacing and controlling. It takes courage to pioneer new emotional territory and then practice until you perfect and master your objective. Specializing in being you is worth the value of your time and investment.

Consider the benefits of taking time to heal, hear, and head toward positive thoughts about yourself that don't include your mistakes from the past. This is a place for initiating your personal rhythm of grace. In other words, have compassion for yourself. You are worthy. This will build a strong foundation for activating personal change that leverages the past instead of impedes your social and emotional progress. Your old emotional defaults will not suffice as a basis for the healthier, wiser times ahead.

You are worthy.

Recognize that life doesn't owe you anything; however, you do owe yourself the energy it takes to give it all you've got to build your life beyond every limitation: There was a time when the world experienced hardships ranging from the serious (death, illness, lost jobs, isolation) to the superficial (missed vacations, cancelled celebrations). Here's the lesson: life doesn't owe you anything—not good health or good fortune or an island vacation in Ibiza. You can work very hard to get the job of your dreams and still lose it. You can beat cancer only to develop it again. The entitlement of believing that life owes you something for your suffering is an easy trap to fall into because you relinquish control over your own destiny to others, or mere circumstances and situations. Bad things happen to good people every day. You have to acknowledge it, let it go, embrace change and then move on with intention and an unyielding passion to live. Hold fast to the law of reciprocity until you've sown good thoughts, words, and deeds and it yields a harvest of good returns.

This realization is liberating because it can help you appreciate your role and responsibility in creating your own happiness, accomplishments, and emotional well-being despite what's happening around you or to you. This is not an admission to ignore reality, but rather the choice to move forward where you can and because you can. There is an end to everything—happiness and suffering alike. You have your entire life ahead to take advantage of every opportunity you create and those presented in life one day at a time. The choice is yours.

Know yourself: It all boils down to your core values and understanding your value, doesn't it? They're the foundations of what guide your decisions and keep you on your path. Think deeply about what makes you tick. Where and what gives you inner fulfillment? Where could you improve your skills? What are you good at? What does life look like when you choose to live by your core values, and by what you see is the best way to live among your family, society, in relationships, and professionally? How will you awaken from a dream to the true vision you have for your life?

Take the time to get to discover, acknowledge, and
internalize your core values and learn how to make
decisions based on those values. Be honest with
yourself about who you are, what you believe in,
and how you behave and react in your daily life, and
adjust where necessary so you are living true to your
values. That means admitting to yourself when and
where you get it right or where you make mistakes,
and take the action to accept the win or correct
the losses. Think about how your temperament
filters how you interpret and perceive your current
circumstances, and how you behave under the
constant pressure of life. Being truthful with yourself
might not be easy, but you're worth it. You're not one
in a million—*you're a one and only.*

You're not one in a million—you're a one and only.

Part Two:

Accept
Your Truth

*L*earning the value of your value means being truthful to yourself and not depending on unhealthy patterns to soften the blow. Trusting your intuition and living your values are critical to your growing self-empowerment and self-confidence. Accepting your truth for what it is, and not how you choose to see it, is more than a process, it's a practice.

Now that you're exploring your core values, you're realizing that how you cope with life's ebbs and flows—health, job, finances, relationships, etc.—is defined by how you accept, personify, and behave according to your core values and understanding of your value. It's time to identify and internalize the **value of your value** so you can continue to build beyond where you are now. How you work toward your personal and professional goals after your world has drastically changed, how you learn to direct your future, and how you walk from here all hinge on you.

Sometimes when you look into the mirror, you discover that you might be holding you back. Maybe you're not living up to your true potential, don't give yourself enough credit for your accomplishments, have ignored your gut instincts, or made big mistakes that have gotten you into a tough situation. It can be difficult accepting hard truths, especially if you've been feeding yourself the line everything is fine when it's really not fine. Why settle for less than what you are capable of?

Internalize the Value of Your Value

When you know and accept the value of your value, you walk your journey confidently and with purpose because you know your worth and are assured in your abilities and potential. When the world around you changes, you can adapt with flexibility because you are confident in who you are. Living your core values and knowing your own value are inexorably linked. When you're living aligned to your values, you make decisions with self-assurance because you are living your truth. You know you're living your best life with your best interests in mind. You're not overconfident or arrogant or boastful, but you know your worth—and you don't settle for a life less than you deserve.

However, when you're down or depressed, battling an illness, under- or unemployed, traumatized, or in any number of circumstances that do not align with your personal values, it is easy to lose your confidence and fall into despair and self-doubt. Defining who you are at heart and what your intentions are at steels your resolve when times are tough. This resolve acts as a guidepost to help you recover faster and rebuild better.

Value your value.

Know Your Worth

Recognizing your self-worth is a big part of accepting your truth. Think about how you view yourself and what you're capable of. You are what you believe you are and what you have to offer. What are you good at? What do you enjoy most? What are you passionate about? When you live your core values and follow your gifts, you strengthen your self-worth because you are living authentically. You build experience and gain confidence by doing things you're good at. Be confident in your awesomeness!

When outward appearances of "success" like material things, wealth, physical appearance start to sway your opinions of yourself is when it's time to buckle down and connect to your core values. It's easy to get caught in the trap of believing what society dictates is the right thing for you. Hinging your self-worth on material things or temporary satisfaction is doing yourself a disservice because they are not permanent. What you get you can always lose, for example saving for years to buy a car that all your friends envy and then having your teenager wreck it. Material goals are subject to the mercies of the world, and while achievable in the short-term, are unsustainable in the long-term. I'm not saying it's bad to have nice things and value their worth, but don't make the mistake of putting the value of material things over your own core values. Judging your self-worth based on what society or other influences determine as "success" is not living your truth. Don't deceive yourself. Self-worth and self-value come from within you, not from things. You determine and set a course for the direction of life by your thoughts, words, and deeds, and how you think about yourself. That is central to being authentically yourself with no apologies or regrets.

I'd be remiss if I didn't offer a word of advice here: if you're having great difficulty recognizing your self-worth or believe you don't have any, I implore you to seek professional help. Sadly for some of us, life has dealt us some powerful punches that are very difficult to recover from. If you find yourself unable to realize your self-worth or don't believe in yourself—and trust me, you have worth and have gifts to offer yourself and others—then it's time to find the courage to speak to someone you can trust about your troubles. There's no shame in admitting you're struggling—on the contrary, there's true power in it. Get some help so you can tap into your inner strength because it's in there somewhere. It's a game changer once you recognize your self-worth and the value you have and who you've yet to become.

Your Emotional Bank Account

I was recently surfing Investopedia to broaden my knowledge about the financial markets when I hit upon the Five Cs of Credit: character, capacity, capital, collateral, and conditions. I made the connection that these five concepts can also apply to our emotional bank accounts. From all the adjusting, pivoting, and tumult we endured until now—and especially through the pandemic—our emotional bank may require a few deposits. We train our brains to think a certain way ultimately to protect ourselves. Adopting a survival mentality is okay when you need to survive but maintaining a constant state of hypervigilance is unhealthy for not only your body, but also your mind and spirit. By applying the Five Cs to your self-worth, you can Build It Beyond to grow your self-worth, much as I have for my own life:

- I am of good **character**, moral fortitude, and determination. I remember speaking with my dear sister friend Wendy L. Alexander, a woman of true character and conscience. She is noteworthy in her influence to inspire entrepreneurs to imagine more for their businesses globally. However, what is impressive is Wendy does not offer flowery words that mislead individuals to believe they are ready when they are not. What would you do and how would you think if you are faced with a decision to tell a high-paying client that you are not ready? Worthy, yes, ready...not yet. Having character means not taking advantage of others while seeking advantages for yourself. You reveal your character and self-worth when making choices for your life.

- I am filled with **capacity** for more than I can imagine. I am actively pursuing the vision for my life and lifestyle that includes giving and receiving in a healthy and sound way that supports my well-being and also that of others around me. What is your capacity for life? Within my sister-friend community of IBH Sister

Sounds World, we have our own bling artisan, Mary Jane Henderson, who takes ordinary items and makes them extraordinary. Mary Jane began blinging items as a hobby and, in the community of "like-minded" women who celebrate their uniqueness, was inspired to build her business beyond what she saw for herself. She had incredible capacity stored within her talent and imagination. Celebrities, neighbors, business clients enjoy the talent of Mary Jane, a woman who shows her capacity, character, commitment, and kindness through her talent that once was her hobby. I offer this example because I want you to search out yourself as an adventurer and discover just how much capacity you have to create something special and unique, as you truly are.

- My relationship with myself is highly valued **capital**. I view and accept it as an abundance of opportunity and emotional and spiritual wealth. I am relational and not transactional in my existence. I share my life and do not sell it as human capital.

My character, integrity, and stature are my capital gains. There is no gift more valuable than the gift of life, the best capital you'll ever have. If you were to ask Nena R. Springs of Sheamixology and Kim Rome the value of celebrating life, each would show you more than they could ever say. The words "success in silence" and "live the difference" represent the passion that these two women demonstrate by living victorious, powerful lives daily. Both freely shared with me by living through their passion and purpose how they survived cancer. They love life with self-care and self-love, and without restraint. You would not want to complain in their presence! These ladies live for the power found in celebrating the present! Your relationship with yourself is purely yours to define. Its true value is realized when you have a passion to live! Create time for self-discovery, you are worthy of the celebration. Silence all doubt and ignite your SHINE!

- Loving God, myself, and others in my life are my **collateral** for success, sustainable relationships, and good decision making. I am prudent and adhere to wisdom and sound counsel. I have a friend, also named Anita, whom I met eons ago. You know that special friend where days and months can go by before you connect again, and when you do you pick up right where you left off? With the Anitas, time stands still and awaits our return. We know the value of the sisterhood collateral between those moments, times of laughter, tears, and overcoming fears. Its irreplaceable and non-negotiable. Who means that much and more to you? You are worthy of healthy, wholesome, and honorable relationships. Give yourself the gift of friendship by being a good friend. Are you willing to believe and experience the beauty of giving without condition? You are worthy of healthy, irreplaceable relationship with others. Who and what represents collateral to you?

- These all represent my **conditions** for engagement of any kind. Timing is important, but for me, trust has extraordinary value and establishes the purpose, amount, and the ongoing investment I have in myself as well as other human lives, agreements, partnerships, and relationships. I understand the value of trusting myself first, and then others. Trust is earned and not given without condition. The precious gift of trust in oneself, talents, and truth are equally matched by the trust you offer others. More importantly and in few words, can you trust yourself? Who can you trust? What are your conditions?

Are you willing to hear more, see more, and reimagine yourself? Will you allow someone to push you out of your comfort zone and into discovery? What are your five Cs that will prompt you to Build It Beyond? Write your Five Cs of Self-Worth here:

- **Character:** _____

- **Capacity:** _____

- **Capital:** _____

- **Collateral:** _____

- **Conditions:** _____

Remember the Five Cs when you have challenges achieving your potential because your emotional bank account is low.

Know Your Worth Exercise

Step 1: Choose a specific challenge that leads your thoughts, communications, and behaviors away from your core values: Identify what about that challenge makes you doubt your trust in yourself and your ability to keep your word to yourself, others, or whatever the circumstance demands your attention. Take today to really zone in and choose an area where you recognize the timing is right to address your concern. When you land on it, write it down on a piece of paper. This part is important.

Step 2: Focus on your goals and aspirations that align with your core values: Remember, your values should guide how you live a life that is true to who you wish to be. Write them down on a separate piece of paper.

Continuing on my experiences, I wanted to honor my value of commitment and build a mindset for completion, instead of competing with the multitude of other things vying for my attention. I wrote down "Commitment to Completion" as my goal, and I envisioned myself completing the project I was working on without getting sidetracked.

Over time, I recognized that there's a world full of experiences happening without me or my influence. The only competition I had is with myself. All the advertising and marketing in the world would never benefit my business or professional or personal relationships if I trained myself to lose well, if I stuck with the outcomes of good decisions that went bad, became comfortable with mediocre results, or became less than I was capable of.

Step 3: Create a personal declaration and covenant to yourself with your intentions: Pick a quiet place to establish a safe and cooperative environment where you can be vulnerable with yourself. Be intentional about this and plan your time, away from distractions. Allow yourself the freedom to feel hope and well-being. End your declaration with the statement "I am a one and only." Announce to yourself,

There is no duplicate of me anywhere in the world. I am not just one in a million. I _____ (fill in your name) am a one and only.

Treasure this personal declaration and the intentions for yourself by silently reading it again repeatedly, until you feel it seep in. Place it where you will see it often. You are bathing your mind and consciousness with truth; allow yourself to feel the results of disciplined thoughts and determined actions to be as dynamic as you were created to be.

Step 4: Trust the Five Cs of your worthiness: If you haven't identified yours, revisit the sidebar above to complete them. Read them silently and slowly and repeatedly to internalize your thoughts of worthiness. This is an important moment.

Step 5: Take a Bath: Although taking a bath is not an option for many people for a wide number of reasons, stick with me here and make the adjustments where necessary. Bathing is an outward expression of an internal change—an emotional or physical cleansing. Cleansing in water in many religious doctrines, from Christianity (baptism) to Judaism (mikveh), symbolize ritual purity. Even the act of preparing for some personal spa time can help you release any emotional or external burdens. As you prepare, be quiet and allow your mind to accept how you see yourself. You are washing away the old and refreshing yourself in preparation for good things to come. As you set out items that help you relax, like essential oils, candles, or bubble bath, also get the paper on which you wrote your challenges. You are going to get the paper wet—it is all part of releasing what troubles or burdens you.

As you soak, run the shower so the water lightly flows over your head, shoulders, and entire being; reflect on the challenges written on the paper. Watch the ink run and the paper disintegrate and get soggy and ruined. Renounce everything that challenges you and announce that it is no longer a part of your life, thoughts, words, or deeds—just like that soppy, wet paper you're holding onto. You are worthy to celebrate, be restored to social and emotional innocence, and open to grow in the way that is your best and best for you.

When you are ready, crumple the paper into a ball and set it aside. Unstop the tub but let the shower continue to run, allowing your challenges to drain away along with the water in your tub. You have allowed yourself symbolically to become completely purified from what holds you back. Be clear, the reality of this act takes place as you accept your new mindset. Align yourself with new practices that are consistent with your empowering beliefs on an ongoing basis.

See this time of purification as the moment where you intentionally let go of your troubles and embrace

who you truly are created to be. As you receive
the transformation, you acknowledge that you are
worthy. As the water recedes, so does your link to
past behavior and thoughts regarding your challenge.
Discard the paper and enjoy the refreshing shower
of your newness. Aristotle said, "We are what we
repeatedly do." You are worth the investment. Your
habits and behaviors create neural pathways in your
brain. The frequency of the behavior establishes the
new foundation for the new results important to you.

"We are what we repeatedly do."

—Aristotle

Take one day at a time and establish the lifestyle changes with consistent small decisions and actions that will impact the quality of the rest of your life. Essentially, when you change your mindset you will change your choices.

Step 6: Declare verbally, aloud: "I am worthy!" Shout it out if it makes you feel better. This is a day of settled and certain resolve! Embrace your worthiness:

- Of the change you want for yourself
- To love and to be loved
- To succeed
- To have and share abundance
- To be protected and protect what is important to you
- To give and receive
- To enjoy self-care because it is true self-love
- To celebrate and be celebrated
- To give and receive support
- To forgive and be forgiven

- To challenge others when they need to be challenged and be challenged for your own sustainable growth

These shout-outs will grow as you grow. Your time has arrived where you recognize remaining the same is a greater risk than being who you are born to be. It is okay to allow yourself to be you.

Step 7: Say these words lovingly and in a low tone for rest and an atmosphere of quietude:
I am not guilty, but rather I was not aware of my uniqueness. If I had known that I was a one and only—created without regret and wonderfully crafted and curated with the intent to inspire, impact, and leave an imprint in the conscious and lives of others—I would have lived out loud long ago. I now know I am innocent and can no longer blame myself or allow things seen or unseen to weigh me down. I am innocent and continue my life free from guilt or shame from this day forward. I can be heard when I whisper knowing that what I contribute is valuable. I understand the value of my value and the

rhythm of accomplishment that lives freely within
me. I am _____*! (fill in your*
name)

Know Your Potential

What do you see as your potential? You have the
potential to go from here to beyond if you set your
mind to it. Don't spend your life blind to your true
potential and shortchanging yourself because you
don't believe in your own abilities. Ignoring your
potential sets you up for undervaluing yourself and
paves the way for others to do the same. That will
only breed frustration, self-pity, and self-criticism.
Your potential lives within you and you need to
recognize it in order to take yourself to the next level.
You owe it to yourself to see yourself honestly for
who you are and what you're capable of. Remember
that your self-worth and potential are not determined
by others. If you are struggling, try asking someone
you trust or seek professional assistance to help you
recognize your potential.

I will always remember chatting with two sister friends Arita Gilliam and Carlene Parkinson in Pittsburgh, Pennsylvania. They are true friends who demanded that I clarify for myself the true value of my investment in the goals of others. They did this by insisting that I sit with them, write down everything I had done to ensure the success of a project we were working on together. Once I had completed the list of tasks fulfilled, to my surprise, it was three pages filled with accomplishments. I sat there amazed at the level of excellence exemplified in completing the tasks. Here is the clincher: the administrative and consulting skills came to me completely naturally and with ease. My dear friends assigned a monetary value to the work and a competitive title to my effort so that I could have a true picture of my value to others and potential for myself. I encourage you to do the same. Start with what is already in your archive of achievement. Interview yourself and discover just how amazing you really are. Then do something special with it.

The second step to knowing your potential is knowing and then living from your value. You'll hear me say this a lot, but that's only because I think it's really important. Knowing the value of your value is the lens through which you view yourself, others, and the world around you. When you are living according to what is important to you, a clear and concise understanding of your contribution boosts your sense of well-being and gives meaning to your life.[1] Think about areas in your life where you are living true to your values and value. Which values speak to you the most? Are you doing everything you can to align with those values? For example, maybe lifelong learning is one of your core values. Are you learning something new every day? Maybe kindness is one of your core values, and you're making sure you bless others, yourself included, with acts of kindness every day. Let your internal compass guide you to the values you cherish most and use that guidance to live up to your potential.

---

2 Veage, S., Ciarrochi, J., Deane, F. P., Andresen, R., Oades, L. G. & Crowe, T. P. (2014). Value Congruence, Importance and Success in the Workplace: Links with Well-Being and Burnout Amongst Mental Health Practitioners. *Journal of Contextual Behavioural Science* 3 (4): 258–264.

Next is evaluating your strengths. Everybody has strengths and weaknesses, but the mistake many of us make is to emphasize our weaknesses or minimize or apologize for our strengths. Do not apologize for who you are and do not apologize for what you are good at doing. It is up to you to toot your own horn!

Do not apologize for who you are and do not apologize for what you are good at doing.

When you acknowledge your strengths and validate yourself, you are recognizing your potential. You are not defined by your weaknesses and your weaknesses should not limit your potential. A strong community or tribe insulates you from isolation. Call upon your friends and family as a lifeline to support you in areas in which you lack confidence or require accountability. We all need support at times; it enrichens our life experience.

We all make mistakes and learning from them is an experience-builder—the key is trying not to repeat those mistakes. When you fail at something it's easy to tell yourself you can't do it and then keep believing that story the next time you're faced with a challenge. When you give yourself the benefit of faith by believing in your strengths, something wonderful happens—you discover you can. With every success, your confidence in yourself and your potential grows. You find success fits you like a well-tailored suit. Every mistake you make is a lesson and an opportunity for you to grow and discover what it feels like to win.

Most importantly, know that your potential is intangible and limitless. It boils down to your mindset and whether you're willing to get uncomfortable stepping out of habits to live up to what you're truly capable of. Adopting a growth mindset frees you from self-limiting beliefs, and the only thing stopping you is you.

Know Your Potential Exercise

What do you see as your strengths?

What do you enjoy doing?

Are you giving yourself the benefit of faith in yourself and intentions? Why? Why not?

Are you prepared to "own" what you are good at doing?

Know Your Boundaries

Boundaries are healthy expressions of how you treat others and how you wish others to treat you. They are the mark of reciprocal relationships and manifestations of what you stand for. You set your boundaries by how you live your core values.

Knowing what you stand for and what behaviors you're willing to accept will help you identify your personal physical, emotional, mental boundaries. Think about what makes you uncomfortable or stressed, and use those feelings to guide where you draw your lines. The more discomfort you feel in a situation, the more your boundaries tend to be stretched. Practice creating and teaching others about your cooperative environment through what you allow and what boundaries you have established.

Temperament plays a big part in boundary setting. For example, imagine your temperament leans toward the melancholic—introverted, detail-oriented, rule follower—and an extroverted sanguine-type gets in your space and talks your ear off for a long time. You may feel uncomfortable or awkward. That's a sign you're stretched beyond your boundaries. Also, consider cultural and communication differences when declaring your boundaries because what's disrespectful for one person may be a healthy way of expressing differences to someone else. In those moments, it is healthy to express your boundaries with civility and empathy. By allowing others to step over your boundaries, you run the risk of compromising your own well-being for the sake of not rocking the boat. At times like these, you must ask yourself which is most harmful to you. What next steps can you take to build communication and strengthen the exchange so your value is no longer compromised?

Your past may be an obstacle in how you establish and enforce your boundaries. For example, if you were raised to be a rule-follower or caretaker, you may have compromised some of your boundaries out of obligation or for praise. Overlooking your own needs for those of others is a recipe for burnout. You may even begin to feel resentment if you believe you're being taken advantage of or being used. You may feel guilty for not meeting someone else's expectations or you may feel out of control by having someone else impose their values on you. Remember, speaking out is the kind thing to do for yourself. You shouldn't be put in a position to leverage your boundaries for someone else's happiness or comfort. If there's not a healthy reciprocity in your relationships, it's time to revisit them and declare your boundaries.

Speaking out is the kind thing to do for yourself.

I often say you learn how to lose well and look good doing it. This means you know how to keep face in tough situations, but you also stand strong in your values and boundaries. It does not mean you get used to stretching your boundaries and get used to settling for less. You give yourself grace to enforce your own boundaries because knowing yourself and what you're willing to accept is critical for your own peace of mind, but it also means you're direct in asserting your boundaries. Notice I said direct—not aggressive, rude, offensive, or apologetic. You can still maintain your decorum and graciousness and still get your point across.

Beware that losing well sometimes can condition you to create self-imposed barriers, and those kinds of barriers can stop you from building beyond where you are now. Self-imposed barriers are behaviors that you may adopt after an upsetting experience that you felt helpless to change. For example, stinging from a bad breakup? You decide dating is not for you. Set off the fire alarm when you burned that holiday dinner? Hosting dinner parties is off your list forever. When we experience negative events, we develop habits to avoid them in the future. Psychologist Martin Seligman called these behaviors learned helplessness. Here's a little secret: you are not helpless, and you have the power within yourself to change for the better.

You can gently but firmly express your boundaries. Here are some words you can use when expressing your boundaries:

- "I know you expect me to have boundaries…"
- "I'm uncomfortable with this. Can we try…"
- "Respectfully, here's why I disagree…"

When you practice asserting your boundaries, you're being genuine to your core values, and living true to yourself.

Learn how to lose well and look good doing it.

Knowing Your Boundaries Exercise

What behavior makes you uncomfortable?

How do you react when someone breaches your boundaries?

What behavior do you consider unacceptable?

How do you express your boundaries?

How do you think your past experiences affect how you set boundaries?

What support do you require to effectively outline your boundaries and execute them?

How important are boundaries to you? And what steps are you prepared to take to follow through?

Do you believe setting boundaries increases your worthiness? Why or why not?

Accepting Your Truth
to Move Beyond

Have you been feeding yourself a line that everything is okay even though it's not? Are you distorting the facts of your situation to sugar-coat your truth? Have you made some poor choices and now face the consequences? We often get stuck in a comfort zone and sometimes that can be harmful to our growth as human beings. Change is scary and unknown. It often means we need to break a bad habit, alter our routine, make a change in a relationship, and (here's the hard one) come clean with ourselves and recognize and start living our truth. You do not value your value when you lie to yourself to soften the blow of a mistake. Neither are you living your truth when a good decision goes bad and you take the fall. Both are divisive and the opposite of your living your truth.

When you're trapped in the story of who you tell yourself you are, you may feel trapped into thinking that's who you will always be. It doesn't have to be that way. It's liberating to have agency over how you think of yourself, and how you direct your future.

When you are capable of shifting your thoughts toward a more positive outcome, you are capable of changing yourself and your circumstances. You are the hero of your own story and you get to decide what happens next.

You have the power to re-create your existence. Once you realize that there is nothing that will hold you down except for you, you'll be in a better place to identify why you feel this way; only then can you create a plan to move forward. You don't have to continue to make the same mistakes over and over again. It's easy to feel defeated when the chips are down and you stay stuck in your comfort zone, but is what you're currently doing satisfying you? Are you living your truth? Are you the best version of you that you can be? That's where your true growth begins— when you admit to yourself that you got yourself where you are, and you are the only one who can change your life. Ask yourself if what you're doing is helping you achieve your goals. If not, it's time to try something else. Change happens out of desperation or inspiration, and that looks different for everybody.

You are the hero of your own story and you get to decide what happens next.

You've got to begin where you are: how do you feel about your current situation? Do you feel defeated, deflated, or uninspired? How do you react when something bad happens? Do you retreat into yourself? Do you grab the nearest pint of ice cream? Do you seek help from others? How you make your changes is influenced by your temperament, your past experiences, and often how you grew up. There's one common thread in all this: you. In order to move beyond, you've got to be honest with yourself and seriously consider your next steps.

Remember above when I talked about self-limiting boundaries? Those are born out of our past negative experiences. We create our own little safety nets of security when we've been burned in the past. Same with how we grew up. If we grew up in a nurturing environment with plenty of encouragement and love, we may be more self-confident and willing to take a risk. But if we grew up in a dysfunctional environment with insecurities such as food, safety, or shelter, then we may tend to be more risk-averse and choose the safe or comfortable route in life. When dysfunction is all you know, you don't know what you don't know. Change can be super scary but that doesn't make it any less necessary for your growth.

I'll share a story from when I was a young girl. I often felt threatened in school because when I'd give the right answer in class, I knew I'd have a fight waiting for me outside the classroom doors. It wasn't cool to be the smart kid with the right answers. I had to learn to get past those lessons of silence for self-protection in order to succeed in sharing my voice, talents, and gifts. With the support of my family and my teachers, I achieved high grades. But it was later in life that I actually released myself to have a confident voice. As an adult, in many situations I gave myself grace to allow myself that win and to allow myself to feel and experience differently. My new attitude is ever increasing daily and brings in a newfound confidence that continuously resonates in me. I now inspire other women to do the same.

Remember this little shorthand: when you Operate with Knowledge, it's okay to be OK. Accepting your truth is operating with knowledge—the knowledge of who you are, what you stand for, how you value your value, and know your truth. You can recognize and accept the tools you already have in yourself to achieve your personal and professional goals.

It's so important to be truthful to yourself to get a realistic view of your life or current situation. Sometimes that means admitting to yourself that a good decision can go bad, or you were wrong, or that you made a poor decision for whatever reason. If your filters are getting in the way, you are not listening. Let go of defensiveness that protects your ego. It's okay to admit when you've made a mistake; just say you're sorry to yourself, then commit to doing something differently. Own your mistakes. Make them right if you can. Stop beating yourself up. Forgive yourself. Then make a better decision next time. You must give yourself grace and forgiveness for your mistakes and the wrongs done to you or others. Life is not perfect, but there's always room for grace toward yourself, which is critical to moving forward and building beyond. You don't have to feel guilty for wanting a better life for yourself.

When you operate with knowledge, it's okay to be OK.

**Facing and Acknowledging Guilt
Without It Interfering In Your Life**

1. Changing for the better
2. Knowing your worth
3. Moving on
4. Protecting your peace
5. Staying true to your vision

Accepting Your Truth Exercise

Think about a situation where you made a poor choice. What was the result? Did you ruminate on the fallout or did you give yourself grace and move on?

If faced with a similar situation, what do you think can be the difference in your response now?

Name two things you could change about your current situation. What would you have to do to make that happen?

Name a time when you were not truthful with yourself. Explore your feelings, then give yourself grace and forgiveness to let it go.

You don't need permission to be you and you don't have to apologize for your strength. Accepting your truth is vital to living your best life. Knowing your value helps strengthen your self-confidence; that propels you forward and gives you assurance in yourself and your abilities. If you don't like how you're living, you are the only one who can make a change. You must know the value of your value and where your potential lies. You can't maximize your self-value without self-awareness and self-forgiveness. Accept your previous not-so-great decisions and resolve to move ahead from where you are now by living, acting, and behaving according to your true values.

Part Three:

Embrace
Your Worth

*S*ituations occur every day where you invest your time, energy, and resources on the wrong audience or initiatives. Your words or deeds are met with a lack of interest, success, or even blank stares! The emotional fallout you experience can leave you frustrated or even angry—at the situation, outcome, other person, or even yourself—for wasting your breath and your precious energy. You think you're doing all the right things...but are you?

Embracing your worth is learning that how and with whom you share your value is a reflection of your thoughts, patterns, and ingrained behaviors. It's okay to be selective with whom you share your pearls of wisdom. Not everyone is the right audience at the right time, and you don't have to be all things to all people.

In any relationship or effort where you may be questioning why you didn't get the outcome you originally hoped for, you might want to begin with questioning your internal dialogue and motivation. Trust yourself and love yourself into a new way of thinking that aligns with your core values and healthy choices, mindset, and lifestyle. Take your time and think about what you want, write it down, read it, rehearse it until it becomes real!

It begins with you. Take ownership of your intentions, behaviors, and actions. Take back your pearls. Embrace your worth.

Punch the Pig

There is a proverb in the Bible (Matthew 7:6) that states "Do not give what is holy to the dogs, nor throw your pearls before swine, lest they trample them under their feet and turn around and attack you."[2] In plain-speak, it means don't waste your words, worth, value, or talents on those who won't appreciate your efforts or who will misunderstand your message.

My take on this parable is "Punch the Pig." Now don't get me wrong, I love animals and would never encourage harming another creature! I don't mean this literally. This is my interpretation of an age-old scripture, but the meaning is universal and timeless. "Punch the Pig" is not about a person, but instead is a challenge to the "giver"—that's YOU—to clarify your value, worth, and willingness to engage in healthier relationships and decisions for yourself and others. The key takeaway here is recognizing how and with whom you share your value and worth may be a reflection of your thoughts, patterns, and ingrained behaviors. Your internal motivations or

3 Modern English Version (MEV), Matthew 7:6

social-emotional imprint for sharing your worth with the wrong people may be at the heart of the matter. So the question you should be asking yourself is, "Am I embracing my worth by sharing my value with the right people for the right reasons?" The answers may surprise you.

Throughout our childhoods, we pick up thought patterns and habits—our internal motivators—from those around us and from our environments. I believe that each of us learn more through our early childhood experiences and lessons than we realize. These imprints grow with us and influence our ideas, ideals, and ways of looking at life. In many ways, we inadvertently strengthen these unspoken thought patterns because they act as filters on our decisions, behaviors, likes, and dislikes. There's legitimate science behind how repetitive thought patterns establish a well-worn path of signals in our brains that act like a thought superhighway, which influences our behaviors, beliefs, and reactions. Remember the saying "thoughts become words, words become actions, actions become habits"? When we continually do what we've always done because we've always done it that way, we reinforce our patterns—some learned since our early childhood—for better or worse.

It's important to identify what motivates you to "share your pearls" and to take ownership of your behavior before you move forward. In my own life, I identified a social and emotional imprint that was guiding my decisions and behaviors like a silent operating system. I wasn't acting out of a need for approval, but instead followed what seemed "natural" to me. The result was me embracing self-limiting beliefs even though I was experiencing real success—not exactly the idea of being successful!—all because of my internal thoughts and beliefs.

"Punch the Pig" can be thought of as a shortcut to modifying your thoughts and behaviors so you don't repeat unhealthy or unproductive habits. I love a good acronym. They're easy to remember and help drive a message home.

- **PUNCH = Perpetuating Unhealthy Needs, Chatter, and Habits:** "Punch" is looking inward to your honest intentions to stop perpetually repeating unhealthy needs, internal chatter you say to yourself, and ingrained habits that drive you to act in ways contrary to your best interest.

- **THE = Take Hold (of the) Evolution:** Embrace your evolution into a life with a better sense of self-awareness, self-love, self-confidence, and self-appreciation. We are all flawed and it's okay to step away from old habits that do not align with your core values and best interests.

- **PIG = Purposed Internal Growth:** Get curious about yourself! By purposely questioning and investigating your internal motivations for why you do what you do, you can identify your "why" and map a path to better thought patterns and habits so you can enjoy internal growth.

"Punch the Pig" is a place in your mindset where you release old and unhealthy thoughts, patterns, and behaviors. It's that place in your thinking where you trade out the unhealthy for the pearl, the wisdom, and the healthy. Why you do what you do is just as important as what you do. How do you walk from here? How do you overcome the willingness to shrink so others can stand? Why are you no longer able to remain in the bud when blossoming is the only option left, and yet you sabotage your own growth to remain the same, and where uncomfortable has become your new comfort zone? It's time to take your pearl back, acknowledge your intrinsic God-given value and "Punch the Pig"!

Know your intentions! In order to grow, it's okay to acknowledge that some of your thoughts or behaviors aren't healthy for you, and you may be spending your efforts and energies in the wrong areas and with the wrong people. Even transferring the value you have for yourself to others who have not proven they value you is unhealthy and unrewarding. Self-love requires knowing your value. To move forward, you will want to do the following: know your value, live your values, know what you value, and value what you know so that you have a guide for personal growth earmarked for no one else but you. Again, I must say, you are not one in a million, you are a one and only. You are worthy!

Punch the Pig Exercise

Think of a situation in your life right now where you could apply "Punch the Pig." What are the unhealthy thoughts that propel your actions? Use the following breakdown to help you rework your thoughts for a better outcome: Remember, limiting behavior can be traced back to limiting beliefs.

Identify how you Perpetuate Unhealthy Needs, Chatter, and Habits: _____

_____

_____

_____

_____

Identify how you Take Hold of your Evolution:

_____

_____

_____

_____

Identify your Purposed Internal Growth:

_____

_____

_____

_____

Take Back Your Pearl

In step with not casting your pearls—to the wrong people, the right people at the wrong time, or the right people for the wrong reasons—is taking back your pearls. Taking back your pearl means abandoning old and unhealthy attachments to ideals that no longer serve you, and not pursuing self-destructive relationships, interactions, or ambitions because the consequences far outweigh any value you receive from these interactions. You rather accept and engage the ideals, behaviors, and thoughts that mirror your value and values.

Taking back your pearl means abandoning old and unhealthy attachments to ideals that no longer serve you.

What others do with your message is not on you. It's out of your control whether someone wants to listen to what you have to say or is ready for all you have to offer. What is on you, however, is recognizing with whom, how, and when to share your pearls. When you're self-aware and embrace your worth, you're empowered to take action when you need to take back your pearl. It's knowing when to cut your losses without feeling resentful, empty, frustrated, or angry. It is what it is. There's nothing wrong with you when someone doesn't want what you have to offer. Always remember that the common denominator in all situations in which you partake is you. When you embrace your worth and value your value, you gain an awareness of who's ready to accept your truth and who's not.

Maybe you're used to unhealthy patterns, beliefs, or actions—some so ingrained in you that you may be on autopilot and not realize you're hurting yourself by repeating the same behaviors. It's kind of like banging your head into the same wall again and again. It's not a good idea and it causes you harm. Knowing your true intentions, value, and values will help guide you to the best outcome for you. What did you want out of this exchange or effort in the first place? Are your intentions internally motivated for the value you receive or are they given with true empathy for the other person?

I took back my pearl when I embraced the value of my accomplishments and talents, thus liberating and empowering me to proceed with action. I banished my old self-limiting beliefs by taking a risk. Serving a community that was receptive—rather than adhering to the social and cultural norms to serve those with familiarity or my common culture—ignited an opportunity for me to have a global and multicultural impact. Identifying where I was given access helped me clarify who would want my "pearls" and why. It solidified how I perceived myself and to whom I offered my gifts and talent.

"Punch the Pig—take back your pearl" can be used as a strategy to reach your personal goals relative to how you think, the words you use, and the patterns of behavior you've learned through your life's experience. Keeping this lesson in mind, you can reinforce your personal value and worth, and cooperatively engage with others to enhance positive healthier outcomes for everyone involved. By disconnecting yourself from unhealthy attachments to old thought patterns and behaviors, and embracing new thoughts, words, and deeds, you take steps on a path toward healthier behavioral attachments, decisions, and communication.

Take Back Your Pearls Exercise

What are your intentions in an exchange? Do you get the outcome you anticipate? Why or why not?

Do you act on unhealthy thought patterns? Why or why not?

Think of a time when you pursued an exchange for the wrong reasons (self-fulfillment, misguided ambition). Reimagine that exchange but this time, reframe your perspective by abandoning unhealthy attachments to old ideals that no longer serve you. What could have happened?

Meet People Where They Are

Hopefully, it's out of a good heart that you give your pearls. When you're aware of your internal motivation and intentions when you're interacting with others, you embrace your worth by gaining an awareness of where people are and if they're ready to receive what you have to offer. Approach each experience from the position of curiosity of what the receiver needs, rather than a position of authority that you have all the answers to their issues. Respect others for where they are.

Have you ever made investments in the right people but at the wrong time—those who didn't want or weren't ready to receive what you have to offer? Maybe you've heard it said to you or have even said to someone else, "Don't waste your breath, they won't listen." Imagine that someone asked you for advice, and when you gave it, they didn't take it. You may have left that interaction feeling unappreciated, frustrated, or even undervalued. It could be that person wasn't ready for your truth yet—the right person but the wrong time. They didn't want it, couldn't hear it, or were afraid of the consequences if they did.

You will encounter times when people aren't ready to hear what you have to put down. That's okay. They may have some growth of their own to work on. If you're wanting to help or lead, I encourage you to meet people where they are so they're in a place to absorb what is being offered. People aren't ready until they're ready. It takes recognizing that you might not have all the answers to meet others' needs.

People aren't ready until they're ready.

I recently experienced a great example of meeting people where they are. I facilitated a program that included people of all ages, and I noticed the intergenerational casting of pearls that landed flat on the floor. The generation gap is real! Neither generation was listening to what the other had to say; they both stubbornly clung to their viewpoints. The younger generation didn't realize it takes Boomers longer to process information, and the Boomers judged the Millennials for not savoring the moments. Both were right, and both were wrong. I witnessed casting pearls to the right people but at the wrong time! As the session went on, I explained that each generation should consider where the other was at that moment and how their life experiences being a part of that generation set the stage to open the conversation from there. Once they understood the value that they can do better together instead of taking a zero-sum approach, the magic of intergenerational collaboration began. After some deep exchanges, both generations felt connected, appreciative, and a little more understanding of one another.

Meet People Where They Are Exercise

Think of a time when you weren't ready to hear someone else's message. Was the giver meeting you where you were? Did the giver approach from a position of curiosity and discovery or authority?

Remember this experience the next time you share your pearls.

Change Your Mind, You'll Change Your Choices

In any relationship or effort where you may be questioning why you didn't get the outcome you originally hoped, you might want to begin with questioning your internal dialogue and motivation: Was it a matter of casting your pearls toward the wrong efforts, or was your intention or motivation not aligned with your core values? When you love yourself, you'll know it's okay to be a flawed human (we all are!), and you release yourself from the bonds of earlier choices you've made. If you made a mistake, take back your pearl and move on. When you change your mind, you can change your choice of options and direction. By letting go of past failures or missteps, you clear your mind of the mental clutter that clouds you from aligning to your core values; with a clear head, you can make healthier choices that improve your mindset and lifestyle.

Take your time and think about what you want, write it down, read it, rehearse it until it becomes real! That's what Building It Beyond is all about: moving yourself past self-limiting thoughts to soar beyond your dreams of what you originally thought your successful life could look like. Embrace your worth by taking one area at a time; identify what is most important to you in order to begin the journey of becoming who you want to be. Practice makes proficient! Celebrate the small steps you take toward creating new thought pathways that are aligned with the new value equation that fuels a healthier lifestyle. Big changes are made from the sum of small efforts.

Practice makes proficient!

Change Your Mind to
Change Your Choices Exercise

Complete these sentences:

I am (who are you today) _____

_____

_____

_____

_____

I was (who were you before) _____

_____

_____

_____

_____

I shall become (how do you reimagine yourself in the future) _____

_____

_____

_____

_____

Embracing your worth means knowing yourself and your intent in every interaction you have. When you become self-aware, you live aligned to your core values, and your intent reflects those values. You invest your time and energy in the right people at the right time for the right reasons. When things don't work out as you intended, you don't ruminate or pout; you look inward to see if the failure was a result of the choices you made or action/inaction you took. You are selective about who you share your pearls with, and you do not cast them among the wrong people. You love yourself and are honest about the role you play in all your interactions, and know you have the power of choice behind you to make a change when you deem the time is right.

Part Four:

Build Your
Platform

*B*uilding your platform is creating a path toward your goals and taking action. Your core values guide your actions to improve your future. Creating SMART goals that align to your core values maps the direction you take toward a future of your choosing.

Best laid plans, however, can get derailed by circumstance, misdirection, misinformation, and so much more. When you find yourself off-goal, it's time to reframe and adopt an abundance mindset. You reframe your situation by looking at it from a different angle to discover new solutions to your barriers. You adopt an abundance mindset when you embrace the concept that there's enough for all and use it to continue your growth. Challenges can be transformational but only if you see them *as temporary setbacks. You have the potential to persevere toward your goals.*

When disappointment, heartbreak, or failure happen to you, find the lessons in your experience and practice self-care because what does not kill you can kill you (stress, depression, health problems, poor habits, addiction, etc.) if you allow challenges to detour you from your true path. Only you can process your challenges in a healthy way or not. Self-care is not selfish; it is critical to valuing your value!

Setting and Hitting Healthy Goals

If you don't know where you're going, you will end up wherever you land. Goals are your roadmap to get to your desired future. Without a plan, you won't know what to do and when to do it, and you could possibly spend your resources and your precious time spinning your wheels. Your goals belong solely to you and should be based your "why" and not some flashy, sparkly trend. Why are you creating this goal? Why is it important to your future? Why does this goal matter to you? Your "why" originates from your core values. When you behave according to your core values, you are sending yourself and the world the message of your true self that is overflowing with inner peace, fulfillment, satisfaction, and love. Aligning your goals to your core values anchors your focus, decision making, and actions. It's a powerful connection that increases your chances of persevering and succeeding.

Goals are your roadmap to get to your desired future.

You can create a plan to keep your life running smoothly no matter the circumstances. Setting SMART goals will help you build that future of your dreams. SMART goals—Specific, Measurable, Attainable, Relevant, and Time-Bound—are a time-tested way of creating a plan for your future. Here's a quick primer and reminder on creating SMART goals:

- **Specific:** You want to zero in on what you ultimately want. Identify which core value you are aligning to your goal.

- **Measurable:** Identify how you will measure your goals. What data can you collect as evidence you're making progress, and how will you collect it? If you're off-path, determine the point where you need re-evaluate and reset.

- **Attainable:** Don't bite off more than you can chew. By creating attainable goals, you're being realistic on what you can truly accomplish in a given time.

- **Relevant.** Your goals should align to your core values and long-term objectives. How do your short- and long-term goals tie into your core values?

- **Time-Bound:** Set an end date. Be ambitious but realistic in setting a timeframe in which to accomplish your goals. Short-term (weekly, daily) goals are great for keeping your motivation and can add up toward significant long-term goals.

Just like a contractor can't build a house without a blueprint, you'll want to write down your goals so you Build It Beyond with focus and precision. It's easy to fall into the trap of taking on too much too soon, and that's a good way to set yourself up for failure and disappointment. It's perfectly fine to aim high but break your goals into bite-sized pieces that fit into the big picture goal. Breaking down your goals into weekly and daily pieces not only helps you feel like you're moving in the right direction, it shows you are making tiny everyday progress toward your overall goal. Once you write your SMART goal, check on yourself regularly and reassess when you get off track. And just because you're not working on all parts of your long-term plan every single day doesn't mean you can't add them to your plan later. They are just steps you haven't reached yet.

Building your platform takes effort on your part. Take that first step. Believe in yourself because you have a new opportunity every day to become the person you deserve to be. When comedian Tiffany Haddish won a Grammy, it warmed my heart to hear her say, "It's a lot of bumpy roads that you cross...And you just have to believe in yourself as much as you can, and against all odds you say, 'You know what, I'm gonna just put my best foot forward and I'm gonna give the world the best that I got.' Anything is possible."[3] And it is.

The road to achieving your goals is indeed bumpy at times; how you react to detours and roadblocks matters. Being prepared will help you enjoy your journey as you move toward your goals. Prepping for and anticipating the inevitable barriers in advance will help you respond when faced with setbacks.

---

3 Zoe Haylock, "Tiffany Haddish Found Out She Won a Grammy While Filming *Kids Say the Darndest Things*," The Vulture, https://www.vulture.com/2021/03/grammys-2021-tiffany-haddish-wins-best-comedy-album-watch.html.

Learn from your experiences, adjust as necessary, and get yourself back on track. This is the only life you get. You get a clean slate every day. Pay attention to the process as you go along. Celebrate your everyday wins! Because small steps will still get you to the finish line. Your best laid plans can be upended through no fault of your own—life is unpredictable; reframing and adopting an abundance mindset can help how you adjust and get back on track when the road gets bumpy.

Setting and Hitting Healthy Goals Exercise

It's time for you to write down your own SMART goals!

Specific: _____

Measurable: _____

Attainable: _____

Relevant: _____

Time-Bound: _____

*Adapt to change
by reframing
your thoughts.*

On your way to hitting your goals, you are going to find yourself derailed from time to time. Situations and circumstances change; heartbreak and disappointment happen. When you cling too tightly to what you think is best out of habit or fear, or when you listen to the constant loop of "I can't" thoughts in your mind, you're missing other ways to find solutions around what's troubling you. That's the time to use your core values to guide your actions to adopt new ways of thinking. Reframing is a tool that helps you view a challenge as an opportunity instead of something to avoid. Reframing is not a denial; it is a shift in your perspective that will allow you to face life's challenges in new and imaginative ways.

Reframing is not a denial; it is a shift in your perspective.

For example, when a fashion photographer takes a picture, she must adjust her lighting to get the best possible shot. She'll shoot pictures from different angles to get the best view of her subject. By reframing how you look at your situation, you too can shine a new light to unearth viewpoints that were hidden to you all along. What you're looking for may be right in front of you, but you just needed better lighting in order to see it.

You can reframe your negative thought patterns by adjusting how you approach a change. You have the power within yourself to replace negative and unproductive thoughts with positive and productive thoughts. When you catch yourself automatically defaulting to emotional ways of thinking, you're building your awareness of how you think, and can begin replacing old patterns with new and positive ones. By looking at change as an opportunity for growth instead of an unsurmountable challenge that stops you dead in your tracks, you may find new solutions around your barriers. Albert Einstein said insanity is trying the same thing and expecting different results. When you get to the point where you've tried everything and nothing works, it's time to surrender those old, tired patterns and try something new. Ask yourself if you can reframe your experience by looking at your situation differently. For example:

- Lost your job? Instead of worrying, use time to improve your skills with free online classes or a new degree program, or pivot your career in an entirely new direction.

- Gained a few unwanted pounds? Instead of comfort eating, use this opportunity to adopt more mindful habits of healthier eating and incorporate movement into your daily schedule.

- Continually frustrated by the onslaught of negative news? Instead of doomscrolling, take a news and social media break and focus on what you can do to improve your little corner of the world. Do something nice for someone else and begin a pay-it-forward pattern.

Reframing helps you find the silver linings in every cloud that comes your way. It changes "impossible" to "I'm possible." You value your value by finding opportunities to Build It Beyond instead of obstacles that hold you back.

Adapt to Change by Reframing Your Thoughts Exercise

Use this exercise to identify some of your negative thought patterns and reframe them with the opposite thought patterns.

Reframe the following negative thoughts, and add your own in the blanks below.

Negative thought: Bad things always happen to me.

Reframed thought: _____

Negative thought: I can't do it.

Reframed thought: _____

Negative thought: I never get what I want.

Reframed thought: _____

Negative thought: I'll never save enough money.

Reframed thought: _____

Negative thought: _____

Reframed thought: _____

Negative thought: _____

Reframed thought: _____

Adopt an Abundance Mindset

An abundant mindset reflects a world of positivity and a wealth of opportunity, a curiosity to investigate what the world has to offer. Abundance is a belief there's plenty for everyone (whereas the opposite, scarcity thinking, is a belief that there isn't enough or when you focus on what you could lose.) Scarcity thinking can be thought of as abundant negatives— never enough of anything, be it fear, hunger, money, anxiety, you name it. Of course you'll have days when you struggle to find enough time for everything on your to-do list, but instead of being stressed out at what you haven't done, you can find peace and calm by being grateful for everything you've already done. How you think is your choice. Life is not a zero-sum experience; because something good happens does not mean something equally bad has to happen. There is no winning or losing—only learning.

An abundant mindset frees you to see opportunities in every new day. Its' a personal commitment you make to yourself to be your best, do your best, see the best in all you say and do. You can't build your platform on a faulty foundation of bad days. Abundant thinking puts you in the driver's seat instead of the passenger seat and gives you clarity to identify your goals because you believe you can, you will, and there's enough for everyone. It's Building It Beyond!

Consider the following to help adopt an abundance mindset:

Practice gratitude: Everything I've learned about adopting an abundance mindset begins with gratitude. Express gratitude for past excellent and noteworthy events and experiences in your life— socially, professionally, romantically, personally. When you are thankful for what you already have, it's enough. You found satisfaction with the now. You can focus on your wins and progress and no amount of scarcity thinking is going to take that away from you. Gratitude helps you choose to break through, not breakdown when you face challenges. Fear and scarcity thinking hold you back. From having the ability to make smart choices for your life to embracing the idea love is a bottomless well, abundant thinking really has no end.

Look for silver linings: When you look for the positive in a situation, you're more likely to find it. Find the good and lovely in yourself, in others, in your situation. When you continually expect the worst to happen, you're likely to find that, too. When you condition yourself to look for endless possibility in everything you do, you're going to imagine more choices and options for your life. Reframing how you approach a problem changes can shed new light and help you see your situation in a new way. You find what you look for, and you get what you anticipate.

You find what you look for, and you get what you anticipate.

Surround yourself with positive people:
Having a network of people who will be your champions, hold you accountable, and be your loudest cheerleading section is vital to your abundant mindset. The people in our life help shape us, so ask yourself what form do you want to take. Enthusiasm for collaboration and creativity is inspiring and helps propel you forward. Misery is contagious and only holds you back.

Value your value: When you appreciate and internalize your capabilities and self-worth, you are living with an abundance mindset. You focus on your strengths, become confident, and are energized to do more and be more. You recognize your weaknesses, accept them for what they are, and refuse to be limited by them. You capitalize on your strengths and actively work to improve them. An abundant mindset breaks you free from self-limiting beliefs. You can't believe in endless possibility if you place limits on yourself.

Speak your truth: Self-talk can make or break you. You listen to the messages you send yourself, positive or negative. Thoughts eventually become actionable habits. Make your words—to yourself and everyone else—tell the story of abundance and positivity. Share your gifts with others, which reinforces abundant thinking.

Plan ahead: It's okay to be grateful for what you have while you're planning for a better future. Having hopes, dreams, and goals does not negate what you already have. When you act on your plans, you are taking the driver's seat and directing your future rather than passively waiting for it to arrive.

Embrace your curiosity: It's easy to lose sight of how much more there is if we go around thinking we know it all. Abundant thinking means there's always more to learn and more ways to grow. It taps into an enthusiasm for moving past old ways of thinking, a willingness to learn, and a vulnerability to say to yourself it's okay if you don't know it all.

Think up when things look down.

Adopt an Abundance Mindset Exercise

Start a gratitude journal: Every night, write at least five things you're grateful for. The practice will be a stretch at first, but it will get you into the good habit of reflecting on the positive side of your challenges. Oprah Winfrey said, "If you look at what you have in life, you'll always have more. If you look at what you don't have in life, you'll never have enough." Well said, my friend.

Quiet yourself so you can hear: Take time each day to be quiet and peaceful to allow abundance into your life. Look inward and let your values guide your decisions and actions. Enter into rest. Know your default, and if it is scarcity, identify the root of why you think this way. A tired mind can't receive. Make time to pray, journal, meditate, or perform any activity that helps put your mind at rest.

Inventory your scarcity thinking: Make a list of your fears and challenge yourself to reframe them into abundances. Your thoughts are powerful motivators in either direction. When you are feeling anxious or less-than, remember your past successes and embrace that lows are temporary. Your life will have both lows and highs.

Learn something new: Challenge yourself to put aside scarcity thinking that keeps you believing in misinformation, disinformation, no information. Look at where you are lacking and with curiosity, learn, seek training, and explore self-improvement to develop and master skills you don't have. Open your mindset and set your ego aside so you don't take every small defeat as a crushing blow. Challenges are opportunities to learn. Pick up a new hobby, practice a new skill, stay curious.

Self-Care Is Self-Value

When building your platform, you'll need a strong foundation, and that's self-care. Many see self-care as something decadent and luxurious, like sitting in a spa wrapped in a terry-cloth robe getting a facial and a mani-pedi. Some envision self-care as something they have to do even though it's out of their comfort zones, like eating that extra serving of spinach because greens are healthy. Well, friend, self-care is so much more than that.

Self-care is protecting your inner peace and your health, and it is not selfish. It's the caring thing to do for yourself and your own well-being. If you've ever listened to the flight attendant's safety speech when you board a plane, he or she will tell you that in the event of an emergency, put on your own oxygen mask first, then help those around you. Do you know why? You're no use to anyone else if you become incapacitated. Think of self-care like putting on your oxygen mask first.

Self-care is your saving grace when you are stuck in a low place and can barely get out of your pajamas. You can't serve yourself or others from an empty pot when you are run-down, depleted, exhausted, and drained of energy. When you maintain self-care your cup runs over and you remain in a position to be the best person you are capable of being. Share with others out of your emotional abundance and not your lack.

Self-care is not selfish.

By using your core values to build and act on your goals, you are valuing your value by making a plan for your future. Creating values-based goals and making values-based decisions will keep you motivated because you're working toward who you wish to become. It's inspiring. Goals are just a roadmap to get you from a dream to a vision of your life. Setting goals helps you anticipate the inevitable curveballs life will throw your way. You can overcome barriers by reframing how you view change and reimagining challenge as an opportunity. When you abandon self-limiting thoughts by adopting an abundance mindset, you're free to work toward achieving your goals unencumbered. When you move forward with confidence and believe in yourself, you can accomplish more than you ever dreamed. You are worthy so make self-care a priority. Each time you achieve a goal or complete a project, you are strengthening your inner value and belief system in yourself. You're building a better you with each accomplishment, no matter how big or small it may seem at the time.

Conclusion

*D*earest friend, you made it to the end! But it's just the beginning. Now that you've read the book and completed the exercises, you are well on your way to building it beyond your way! What Build It Beyond means to you is as unique as you are. Life is not a one-size-fits-all endeavor.

Your core values are yours and yours alone, and are a reflection of how you recognize your truth. How you channel your truth into your life is up to you. Your values help you stand on firm footing as the world around you swirls in chaos. You are learning to accept your truth, trust your intuition, and embrace the value of your value by not settling for less than you are capable of.

You won't let past or present mistakes hold you back. You celebrate and embrace your worth because you are a one and only! You now know it is okay to be selective with whom you share your pearls of wisdom because you know you don't have to be all things to all people. You are taking ownership of your intentions and behaviors, learning to love yourself first, and are sensitive to the intentions and behaviors of others. Embracing your newfound power helps you create a path toward your goals and helps you adapt when things go sideways. You see challenges as temporary setbacks because you now know you have the potential to weather any storm.

Depending on what healthy choices you make, like giving yourself grace to make missteps, choosing to eliminate scarcity mentality, exploring self-awareness to find peace within yourself, setting goals, and honoring yourself and your values, you can continue to Build It Beyond toward a life of wholeness, fulfillment, and commitment.

Build It Beyond has opened doors to new opportunities for me, and I am hopeful it does the same for you! I invite you to collaborate with me along our journey at IBHimagecentre.org.

Gratitudes

God, thank you. Your eternal presence empowers me to stand, heal and thrive, then release my voice so others would want to experience the same.

Thank you to my beautiful daughter Antonia, you are my constant heartbeat, and I love you to the moon and back. To my granddaughter Amaiah and her dad Leonard, you are my family and living inspiration. Your presence in my life is absolutely everything and always will be.

To my dad, Pastor Charles E. Willis, Sr., Mary McCurdy-Willis (affectionately known as "sweet-one"), and my five extremely handsome brothers and their beautiful wives, your love and prayers have always made the difference in my life. I appreciate you all. To my mom, the late Dr. Velma L. Willis, I will passionately live and laugh out loud in honor and celebratory memory of you.

My travels and service over the years have created a tapestry of wisdom and meaningful appreciation for shared experiences that have influenced my life, strengthened my resolve to Build It Beyond, and support others to do the same. I also salute my IBH Sister Sounds World family; my Arizona, Fort Myers, Virginia Beach, Detroit, Delaware, Texas, and Denver friends; my spiritual sons and daughters; and my colleagues in ministry.

To you who have encouraged me to speak and share answers so others could find their way: Pastor Archie Dennis Jr., Dr. Fredrick G. Sampson, Apostle William Glover, and Bishop Ezekiel Williams. Added to this dynamic group of influencers are Anne Bruce and Phyllis Jask. I thank you all.

Bishop Gilbert Coleman and the late Pastor Elaine Williams, your command to walk in power changed strengthened my focus and life direction. Dr. Arthur Tigney Jr., thank you for being a brother and encouraging me to feel and heal. To my extended family, Rodrick and Natalia Miller, you encouraged me to soar without apology and live worthy of God's intended purpose for my life, thank you so very much.

Most of all, Traci Smith, spiritual daughter and friend, you are an amazing woman of faith and triumph. I am proud of you and thank you for your unmatched sisterhood. Continue to soar! I am always near.

"As I have said before and will forever more, I am not wired for hatred, bitterness, malice, or revenge. I am wired for love, therefore, #Icanlivewithlove and you will too!"

—Anita

About the Author

*A*nita Willis is a dynamic and passionate speaker, author, trainer, and lifestyle/temperament coach as well as the force behind the IBH Image Centre. Anita has spent a lifetime encouraging others to live with authenticity, transparency, faith, courage, beauty, and confidence. She created the Sister Sounds YouTube platform to inspire and encourage women the world over to dig deep, leverage their strength, and share their successes.

As an image enhancement professional specializing in therapeutic skin and body care, Anita learned that the combination of self-care plus client-centered service equaled sales and leadership development success—but only if one recognized the value of their own value. Her three decades' experience taught her how to overcome her own life's adversities, including racial discrimination, sickness, and divorce. With faith and resilience, she has held fast to her vision and value so she can encourage others to be authentic, powerful, loving, and grateful.

Anita skillfully weaves her self-leadership expertise with her own life's experiences to create a tapestry of straight-from-the heart wisdom and inspiration for her audiences.

Anita has a Masters in the Science of Leadership, an international certification in Temperament Therapy and Coaching, and is a graduate of advanced studies through Jelene Institute of Esthetics. She is also an ordained minister.

As one committed to challenging participants to Build It Beyond, Anita teaches that real answers arise only by reflecting your vision, voice, and your value!

Find Anita online at

info@builditbeyond.com

BuildItBeyondCoaching.now.site

build_it beyond_anitawillis

Anita Dawn Willis

Anita Willis IBH

@builditbeyond

A special message from Anita Willis

I hope that my book, *Build It Beyond: From a Dream to a Vision for Your Life*, inspires you to strive toward your dreams and aspirations.

To order signed copies of my books, go to media@builditbeyond.com

 Invite me to speak at your next meeting, workshop, training, or special event. For fees and availability, email me at media@builditbeyond.com or go to BuildItBeyondCoaching.now.site

Let's stay in touch! Please send your stories on how my book and media have affected you or changed your life to awillis@IBHimagecentre.org.

Follow me on social media!

build_it beyond_anitawillis

Anita Dawn Willis

Anita Willis IBH

@builditbeyond